TRIBULATIC

No. 1.—INTRODUCTION.

CHORUS AND QUARTET.

Lord most holy! Lord most mighty!
Righteous ever are Thy judgments.
Hear and save us, for Thy mercies' sake.

No. 2.—AIR.—(Tenor.)

Lord! vouchsafe Thy loving-kindness,
Hear me in my supplication,
And consider my distress.
Lo! my spirit fails within me,
Oh! regard me with compassion,
And forgive me all my sin!
Let Thy promise be my refuge,
Oh, be gracious and redeem me,
Save me from eternal death!

No. 3.—DUET.—(1st and 2nd Soprano.)

Power eternal! Judge and Father!
Who shall blameless stand before Thee,
Or who Thy dreadful anger fly!
Hear, and aid us strength to gather,
To obey Thee, still adore Thee,
In hope and faith to die!

No. 4.—AIR.—(Bass.)

Through the darkness Thou wilt lead me,
In my trouble Thou wilt heed me,
And from danger set me free.
Lord! Thy mercy shall restore me,
And the day-spring shed before me,
All salvation comes from Thee!

No. 5.—RECITATIVE (Bass) and CHORUS.

Thou hast tried our hearts towards Thee; but if Thou wilt not forsake us, our souls shall fear no ill.

Lord! we pray Thee help Thy people; save, O save them; make them joyful, and bless Thine inheritance.

No. 6.—QUARTET.

I have longed for Thy salvation, and my hope was in Thy goodness! Blessed be Thy Name O Lord, for ever!

Now and henceforth, we beseech Thee, turn our hearts to Thy commandments, and incline them evermore to keep Thy law.

Give Thy servants understanding, so that they may shun temptation, and in all things follow Thee.

Oh! vouchsafe us true repentance, teach us always to obey Thee, and to walk the way of peace.

Let Thy light so shine before us,
And Thy mercy be upon us,
Ev'n as is our trust in Thee.

No. 7.—CAVATINA.—(2nd Soprano.)

I will sing of Thy great mercy, for I was in deep affliction, and Thou didst deliver me. I will call unto the people, and the nations all shall hear me, and shall praise Thy holy Name!

No. 8.—AIR (1st Soprano) and CHORUS.

When Thou comest to the judgment, Lord, remember Thou Thy servants! None else can deliver us.

Save, and bring us to Thy kingdom, there to worship with the faithful, and for ever dwell with Thee!

No. 9.—QUARTET.

(*Without accompaniment.*)

Hear us, Lord! We bless the Name of our Redeemer! and His great and wondrous mercies now and ever glorify!

No. 10.—FINALE.

To Him be glory evermore. Amen.

ROSSINI'S STABAT MATER.

No. 1.—INTRODUCTION.

CHORUS AND QUARTET.

Stabat mater dolorosa
Juxta crucem lacrymosa,
  Dum pendebat Filius.

No. 2.—AIR.—(TENOR.)

Cujus animam gementem
Contristantem et dolentem
  Pertransivit gladius.
O quam tristis et afflicta
Fuit illa benedicta
  Mater Unigeniti;
Quæ mœrebat et dolebat
Et tremebat, cum videbat
  Nati pœnas inclyti.

No. 3.—DUET.—(1st & 2nd SOPRANO.)

Quis est homo que non fleret,
Christi matrem si videret
  In tanto supplicio ?
Quis non posset contristari
Piam matrem contemplari
  Dolentem cum Filio ?

No. 4.—AIR.—(BASS.)

Pro peccatis suæ gentis
Vidit Jesum in tormentis,
  Et flagellis subditum.
Vidit suum dulcem natum
Morientem desolatum
  Dum emisit spiritum.

5.—RECITATIVE (BASS) AND CHORUS.

(Without Accompaniment.)

Eia, mater, fons amoris,
Me sentire vim doloris
  Fac, ut tecum lugeam.
Fac ut ardeat cor meum
In amando Christum Deum.
  Ut sibi complaceam.

No. 6.—QUARTET.

Sancta mater, istud agas,
Crucifixi fige plagas
  Corde meo valide.
Tui nati vulnerati,
Tam dignati pro me pati,
  Pœnas mecum divide.
Fac me vere tecum flere,
Crucifixo condolere,
  Donec ego vixero.
Juxta crucem tecum stare,
Te libenter sociare
  In planctu desidero.
Virgo, virginum præclara,
Mihi jam non sis amara,
  Fac me tecum plangere.

No. 7.—CAVATINA.—(2nd SOPRANO.)

Fac ut portem Christi mortem,
Passionis ejus sortem,
  Et plagas recolere.
Fac me plagis vulnerari,
Cruce hâc inebriari,
  Ob amoren Filii.

No. 8.—AIR (1st SOPRANO) AND CHORUS.

Inflammatus et accensus
Per te, Virgo, sim defensus
  In die judicii.
Fac me cruce custodiri,
Morte Christi præmuniri,
  Confoveri gratiâ.

No. 9.—QUARTET.

(Without Accompaniment.)

Quando corpus morietur,
Fac ut animæ donetur
  Paradisi gloria.

No. 10.—FINALE.

In sempiterna sæcula. Amen.

ROSSINI

Stabat Mater

(TRIBULATION)

for soprano, alto, tenor & bass soli, SATB & orchestra

With English Words adapted by William Ball

Order No: NOV 070255

NOVELLO PUBLISHING LIMITED
14/15 Berners Street, London W1T 3LJ

No. 1.

INTRODUCTION.

sf
smorz.
1st Treble. Tutti.
2nd Treble. Tutti.
Tenor (8ve. lower.) Tutti.
sotto voce.
Sta - bat ma - ter do - lo -
Lord most ho - ly, Lord most
Bass. Tutti. sotto voce.
Sta - bat ma - ter do - lo - ro
Lord most ho - ly, Lord most migh
pp
p
sotto voce.
Sta - bat ma - ter do - lo - ro
Lord most ho - ly, Lord most migh
sotto voce.
do - lo - ro
most migh
ro
migh

Soli.
- sa. Sta - bat ma - ter do - - lo - ro - sa
- ty! Lord . . . most ho - ly, Lord . . . . most migh - ty!
Soli.
- sa. Sta - bat ma - ter do - - lo - ro - sa
- ty! Lord . . . most ho - ly, Lord . . . most migh - ty!
Soli.
- sa. Sta - bat ma - ter do - - lo - ro - sa
- ty! Lord . . . most ho - ly, Lord . . . most migh - ty!
Soli.
- sa. Sta - bat ma - ter do - - lo - ro - sa
- ty! Lord . . . most ho - ly, Lord . . . most migh - ty!
p
pp
jux - ta . . . cru - cem . . . la - cry - - mo - sa. . . .
Righ - teous . . e - ver . . . are thy . . . judg - ments. . .
jux - ta cru - cem la - cry - - mo - sa.
Righ - teous e - ver are thy judg - ments.
jux - ta cru - cem la - cry - - mo - sa.
Righ - teous e - ver are thy . . . judg - ments.
jux - ta cru - cem la - cry - - mo - sa.
Righ - teous e - ver are thy judg - ments.

Tutti.
Soli.
Sta - bat ma - ter do - - lo - ro - sa jux - ta . .
Lord . . . most ho - ly, Lord . . . most migh - ty! Hear and . .
Tutti.
Soli.
Sta - bat ma - ter do - - lo - ro - sa jux - ta
Lord . . . most ho - ly, Lord . . . most migh - ty! Hear and
Tutti.
Sta - bat ma - ter do - - lo - ro - sa
Lord . . . most ho - ly, Lord . . . most migh - ty!
Tutti.
Sta - bat ma - ter do - - lo - ro - sa
Lord . . . most ho - ly, Lord . . . most migh - ty!
Tutti. ff
cru - cem la - cry - mo - sa, dum pen - - - -
save us, hear and save us, save us,
Tutti. ff
cru - cem la - cry - mo - sa, dum pen - - - -
save us, hear and save us, save us,
Soli.
Tutti. ff
cru - cem . . la - cry - mo - sa, dum pen - - - -
save us, . . hear and save us, save us,
Soli.
Tutti. ff
la - cry - mo - sa, dum pen - - - -
hear and . . save us, save us,

de - - bat fi - - li - - -
for thy mer - - cies'
us.
sake.
sf
Tenor Solo.
Sta - - bat
Lord . . . most
smorz.
pp

ma - ter do - - - lo - ro - sa jux - - - ta
ho - ly, Lord most migh - ty! Righ - - - teous
Soli.
Dum pen - de - bat,
Hear, and save us,
Soli.
Dum pen - de - bat,
Hear, and save us,
Soli.
cru - cem la - - - cry - mo - sa. Dum pen - de - bat,
e - ver are . . . thy judg - ments. Hear and save us,
dum pen - de - bat.
hear and save us.
dum pen - de - bat.
hear and save us.
Tutti.
dum pen - de - bat, dum pen - de - bat fi - li - us.
hear and save us, save us for thy mer - cies' sake.

TUTTI.
dum . . pen - de - bat, dum pen - de - bat, dum pen -
Hear . . and save us, hear and save us, save us
f TUTTI.
dum . . pen - de - bat, dum pen - de - bat, dum pen -
Hear . . and save us, hear and save us, save us
dum . . pen - de - bat, dum pen - de - bat, dum pen -
Hear . . and save us, hear and save us, save us
f TUTTI.
dum . . pen - de - bat, dum pen - de - bat, dum pen -
Hear . . and save us, hear and save us, save us
SOLI.
- de - bat fi - li - us. Sta - - bat
for thy mer - - cies' sake ! Lord . . . most
SOLI.
- de - bat fi - li - us. Sta - - bat
for thy mer - - cies' sake ! Lord . . . most
SOLI.
- de - bat fi - li - us. Sta - - bat
for thy mer - - cies' sake. Lord . . . most
SOLI.
- de - bat fi - li - us. Sta - - bat
for thy mer - - cies' sake. Lord . . . most

ma - ter do - - - lo - ro - sa jux - ta cru - cem
ho - ly, Lord . . . . most migh - ty! Righ - teous e - ver
ma - ter do - - lo - ro - sa.
ho - ly, Lord . . . most migh - ty.
ma - ter do - - lo - ro - sa jux - ta cru - cem
ho - ly, Lord . . . most migh - ty! Righ - teous e - ver
ma - ter do - - lo - ro - sa jux - ta cru - cem
ho - ly, Lord . . . most migh - ty! Righ - teous e - ver
la - cry - mo - sa, dum pen - de - bat fi - li -
are thy judg - ments: save us for thy mer - cies'
la - cry - mo - sa dum pen - de - bat fi - li -
are thy judg - ments: save us for thy mer - cies'
la - cry - mo - sa dum pen - de - bat fi - li -
are thy judg - ments: save us for thy mer - cies'

ff CHORUS.
us. sake!
Jux - - ta cru - - cem la - - - cry - - -
Righ - - teous e - - ver are thy
ff CHORUS.
Jux - - ta cru - - cem la - - - - cry - - - -
Righ - - teous e - - ver are thy
ff CHORUS.
- us. Jux - - ta . . cru - cem la - cry -
sake! Righ - - teous . . e - ver are thy
ff CHORUS.
us. sake
Jux - - ta cru - cem la - cry - mo - sa, la - cry -
Righ - - teous e - ver are thy judg - ments, are thy
ff
- mo - - - - - - - - - - sa, dum . . . pen -
judg - - - - - - - - - ments: save . . . us
- mo - - - - - - - - - - sa, dum . . . pen -
judg - - - - - - - - - ments: save . . . us
- mo - - - - - - - - - - sa, dum . . . pen -
judg - - - - - - - - - ments: save . . . us
- mo - - - - - - - - - - sa, dum . . . pen -
judg - - - - - - - - - ments: save . . . us

sotto voce.
Tutti. ff
de - bat . . fi - li - us, jux - ta cru - - - cem
for . . thy . . mer - cies' sake ! Righ - teous e - - - ver
de - bat fi - li - us, jux - ta cru - - - cem
for thy mer - cies' sake ! Righ - teous e - - - ver
de - bat fi - li - us, jux - - - ta . .
for thy mer - cies' . . sake ! Righ - - - teous . .
de - bat fi - li - us, jux - ta cru - cem la - cry -
for thy mer - cies' sake ! Righ - teous e - ver, righ - teous
p
pp
ff
la - - - cry - - - - mo - - - - - - - - sa,
are thy judg - - - - - - - - ments :
cru - - cem la - - cry - mo - - - - - - - - sa,
e - - - ver are thy judg - - - - - - - - ments
mo - - sa, la - - cry - mo - - - - - - - - sa,
e - - - ver are thy judg - - - - - - - - ments :

sotto voce.
dum . . . . pen - de bat fi - li - us,
save . . . . us for thy mer - cies' sake!
sotto voce.
dum . . . . pen - de - bat fi - li - us,
save . . . . us for thy mer - cies' sake!
sotto voce.
dum . . . . pen - de - bat fi - li - us,
save . . . . us for thy mer - cies' sake!
sotto voce.
dum . . . . pen - de - bat fi - li - us,
save . . . . us for thy mer - cies' sake!
pp
Chorus.
sotto voce.
do - lo - ro - sa,
Hear and save us,
Soli.
la - crymo - sa,
hear and save us,
Tutti.
p
dum pen -
hear and
Chorus.
sotto voce.
do - lo - ro - sa,
Hear and save us,
Soli.
la - crymo - sa,
hear and save us,
Tutti.
p
dum pen -
hear and
Tutti.
p
dum pen -
hear and
p Tutti.
dum pen -
hear and
f
pp
f
p

- - de - - bat fi - - li -
save us, for . . . . thy mer-cies'

- - de - - bat fi - - li - -
save us for . . . . thy mer-cies'

TENOR SOLO.
fi - - - - - - - li -
for . . . . . thy mer - cies'

- - de - - bat fi - - - - - li -
save us, for . . . . thy mer-cies'

- - de - bat, dum pen-de-bat fi - - - - li -
save us, save us for thy mer - - - - cies'

mf

- - us.
sake!

- - us.
sake!

- - us.
sake!

- - us.
sake!

p

crescendo.

p

p

ff

No. 2. AIR.—"CUJUS ANIMAM."

(LORD, VOUCHSAFE THY LOVING KINDNESS.)

Allegro maestoso.
PIANO.
♩ = 100.
ff
pp
tr
dolce.
ff
pp
pp
TENOR.
p
Cu - - jus a - - - ni - mam ge - men - - tem con - - - tris -
Lord, vouch-safe thy lov - - ing kind - - ness hear me
- tan - - tem et do - len - tem per - - tran - si - - vit
in my sup - - pli - ca - tion, and con - si - - der

gla - di - us. Cu - - - jus a - - - ni -
my dis - tress. Lord! vouch - safe thy
- mam ge - men - - tem con - - tris - tan - - tem
lo - - - ving kind - - ness, hear me in my
et do - len-tem per - tran - si - vit
sup - - pli - ca - tion, and con - si - der
gla - di - us. O quam tris - - - tis
my dis - tress. Lo! my spi - - - rit

et . . . . . af - flic - ta fu - - - it il - - - - la
fails with - in me. Oh! re - gard me
be - - - ne - dic - ta, fu - - - it il - la
with . . . com - pas - sion, Oh! . . . re - gard me
be - - - ne - dic - ta ma - - ter, ma - - ter
with . . . com - pas - sion, and . . for - give, . . for
u - ni-ge - ni - ti, O quam tris - tis
- give me all my sin. Lo! my spi - rit
et af - flic - ta fu - it il - la
fails with - in me, Oh! re - gard me,
sf
pp
p
f
ff

pp
be - - ne - dic - ta ma - - - ter, ma - - - ter
with com - pas - sion. and for - give, for -
sf
p
pp
a piacere. a tempo.
u - - - ni - ge - ni - ti; . . Quæ mœ - re - - bat
- give me all my sin. Let thy pro - - mise
et do - le - - - bat et tre - me - - bat,
be my re - - - fuge, Oh! be gra - - cious
cum vi - de - bat na - - - ti pœ - nas
and re - deem me, save me from e -
f
ff
in - cly - ti, et tre - me - - bat,
- ter - nal death! Oh! be gra - - cious

cum vi - de - - bat na - - ti pœ - nas
and re - deem me, save me from e -

in - - cly - ti, quæ mœ-re - bat et do - le - bat et tre
- ter - - nal death! Let thy pro - mise be my re - fuge; oh! be

- me- bat, cum vi - de - bat, et tre - me - bat, cum vi - de - bat na - ti
gra-cious, and re-deem me, oh! be gra - cious, and re - deem me, save me

pœ - - - - - - - nas in - cly - ti, quæ mœ-
from . . . . e - ter - nal . . death! Let thy

- re - bat et do - le - bat et tre-me - bat, cum vi - de - bat, et tre -
pro - mise be my re - fuge; oh! be gra-cious, and re-deem me, oh! be

cres. .

- me - bat cum vi - de - bat na - ti pœ - - - - - - - - nas
gra - cious, and re - deem me, save me from . . . . e -

in - cly - ti, na - - - ti
- ter - nal . . . death, save me

pœ - - - - - - - - - nas in - cly - ti.
from . . . . e - ter - nal death.

No. 3. Duet.—"QUIS EST HOMO."

(POWER ETERNAL.)

o, si vi-de - ret, si vi-de - ret in tan - to sup-
fly? Who shall blame - less stand be-fore thee, or who thy
f p
-pli - - - - - ci - o? Chris-ti ma - trem si vi-
an - - - - - ger fly? Who shall blame - less stand be-
f pp pp
-de - ret in tan - to sup-pli - ci - o?
-fore thee, Or thy dread - ful . . an - ger fly?
2nd Treble.
Quis non
Hear, and
pos - set con-tris-ta - ri pi-am ma - trem con-tem-
aid us strength to ga - ther, to o-bey thee, still a-
f p
-pla - ri, pi-am ma - trem con-tem-pla-ri do - - -
-dore thee, to o-bey thee, still a-dore thee, and in

- - len - tem cum fi - - li - o, pi - am ma - trem con-tem -
hope and faith to die, to o-bey thee, to a -
p
sf
sf
- - pla - - ri do-len - tem cum fi - - - - - - li - o, pi - am
- - dore thee, in hope and faith to die, to o -
f
f
ma - trem con - tem-pla - ri do - len - tem cum fi - li -
- - bey thee, still a - dore thee, and in hope and faith to
pp
Quis est ho - mo qui non fle - ret, Chris - ti
Pow'r E ter - nal! Judge and Fa - ther! Who shall
- - o? Quis est ho - mo qui non fle - ret, Chris - ti
die. Pow'r E - ter - nal! Judge and Fa - ther! Who shall
f
p
f
ff
ff

ma - trem si vi - de - ret, quis est ho - mo qui non
blame - less stand be - fore thee? Pow'r E - ter - nal! Judge and
ma - trem si . . vi - de - ret, quis est ho - mo qui non
blame - less stand be - fore thee? Pow'r E - ter - nal! Judge and
p f ff
fle - ret, Chris - ti ma - trem si vi - de-ret, Chris-ti
Fa - ther! Who shall blame - less stand be - fore thee? Who shall
fle - ret, Chris - ti ma - trem si vi - de-ret, Chris-ti ma - -
Fa - ther! Who shall blame - less stand be - fore thee? Who shall blame - -
p f p f ff
ma - - - - trem si vi - - de - ret in
blame - - - - less stand be - - fore thee, or thy
- trem si vi-de - - - - - - - - - - -
- less stand be-fore . . . .
p f p
tan - to, in tan - to sup-pli - ci - o? Quis non
dread - ful, thy dread - ful . . . an - ger fly? Hear and
- ret in tan - to sup-pli - ci - o?
thee, or thy dread - ful an - - ger fly?
p

pos - set contris - ta - ri pi - am ma - trem con-tem-
aid us strength to ga - ther, to o - bey thee, to a -
Quis non pos - set con-tris-ta - ri, piam ma - trem
Hear and aid us strength to ga - ther, to o-bey thee,
- pla - ri, quis non pos - set con-tris-ta- ri pi-am
- dore thee, hear, and aid us strength to ga-ther, to o -
contemplari, quis non pos - set con-tris-ta - ri, pi-am
to a-dore thee, hear and aid us strength to ga - ther, to o -
ma-trem . . . con . . . tem - pla - ri, quis non pos - set con-tris-
bey and . . . still . . . a - - dore thee, hear, and aid us strength to
ma-trem . . . con . . . tem - pla - ri, quis non pos - set con-tris-
bey and . . . still . . . a - - dore thee, hear, and aid us strength to
- ta - ri pi - am ma - trem con - tem - pla - ri, quis non
ga - ther, to o - bey and still a - dore thee, hear, and
- ta - ri pi - am ma - trem con - tem - pla - ri, quis non
ga - ther, to o - bey and still a - dore thee, hear, and

pos - set con-tris - ta - ri pi - am ma - trem con - tem -
aid us strength to ga - ther, to o - bey . . and still . a -
pos - set con-tris - ta - ri pi - am ma - trem con - tem -
aid us strength to ga - ther, to o - bey . . and still . . a -
- pla - ri, pi-am ma - - - - trem con - tem - - -
- dore thee, to o - bey 'thee, still a - - -
- pla -ri, pi-am ma - trem con-tem-pla - ri do - -
- dore thee, to o - bey . . and still a - dore . . thee, a - - -
- pla - ri do - len - tem, do - len - tem cum fi - li -
- dore thee, a - dore thee, in hope . . and faith . . to
- len - - - tem, do - len - tem cum fi - li -
- dore . . . . thee, in hope . . and faith . . to

- - o, cum fi - li - o do -
die, in hope and faith, in
- - o, do - - len - tem, do - - len - tem, do -
die, to o - bey thee, a - dore thee, in
sf
sf tr tr
- len - - - - - - - tem cum - fi - li - o?
hope . . . . and . . faith to die.
sf tr tr
- len - - - - - - - tem cum - fi - li - o?
hope . . . . and . . faith to die.
col canto.
dolce.
pp
pp
f p pp ff ff

No. 4

AIR.—"PRO PECCATIS."

(THROUGH THE DARKNESS.)

Pro pec - ca - tis su - - æ gen - tis vi - - dit
Through the dark - ness thou wilt lead me, in my
pp
Je - sum in tor - men - tis et fla - - gel - lis,
trou - ble thou wilt heed me, and from dan - ger,
et fla - gel - lis, et fla - gel - lis sub - di -
and from dan - ger, and from dan - ger set me
f
pp
- tum.
free.
pp
sf
ff

Vi dit su- um
Lord! . . thy mer - cy
sotto voce.
dul - cem na-tum mo - ri - en - tem de - so - la - tum
shall . . re - store me, and . . the day - spring shed . . . be - fore me,
tr
dum. . e - mi - sit spi - ri - tum.
all . . sal - va - tion comes . . from thee.
pp
sf
Vi - dit su - um dul - cem na - tum mo - ri -
Lord! thy mer - cy shall re - store me, and the
- en - tem de - so - la - tum dum e - mi - sit,
day - spring shed be - fore me, all sal - va - tion,

dum e - mi - sit, dum e - mi - sit spi - ri -
all sal - va - tion, all sal - va - tion comes from
tum, vi - dit su - um dul - cem
thee! Lord! thy mer - cy shall re -
na - tum mo - ri - en - tem de - so - la - tum
- store me, and the day-spring shed be - fore me,
dum . . . e - mi - sit, dum e - mi - sit spi - ri
all . . . . sal - va - tion, all sal - va - tion comes . . . from
- tum, vi - dit su - um dul - cem
thee! Lord! thy mer - cy shall re
f
p
mf
ff
tr
sf
pp

na - tum mo - ri - en - tem de - - so - la - tum
- - *store me, and the day-spring shed be - fore me,*

mf *ff* *tr*

dum . . e - mi - sit, dum e - - - mi - sit . . spi - ri
all . . sal - va - tion, all sal - - - va - tion . . comes . . from

sf *sf* *sf* *pp*

- tum, e - - mi - sit, e - mi - sit spi - - ri - -
thee, all, all sal - - - va - - tion comes . . from

ff *tr*

- tum, e - - mi - sit, e - mi - sit spi - - ri - -
thee, all, all sal - - - va - - tion comes . . from

tr

- tum.
thee.

No. 5. CHORUS AND RECITATIVE.—"EIA MATER"

(THOU HAST TRIED OUR HEARTS.)

Andante mosso.
BASS SOLO.
1st TREBLE
2nd TREBLE.
TENOR (8ve. lower).
BASS.
f
E - ia, ma - ter, fons a - mo - ris, me sen - ti - re vim do -
Thou hast tried our hearts to - wards thee; but if thou wilt not for -
PIANO. (ad lib.)
♩ = 76.
Andante mosso.
f
- lo - ris fac, ut . . . . te - - cum . . . lu - - - ge -
- sake us, our souls . . . shall . . . fear, . . shall fear . . . . no

sotto voce.
Fac ut ar - de - at cor me - - um
Lord! we pray thee, spare thy peo - - ple,
sotto voce.
Fac ut ar - de - at cor
Lord! we pray thee help thy
sotto voce.
Fac ut ar - de - at cor
Lord! we pray thee help thy
sotto voce.
Fac ut ar - de - at cor
Lord! we pray thee help thy
sotto voce.
- am.
ill.
Fac ut ar - de - at cor
Lord! we pray thee help thy
mf
In a - man - do Christum De - um,
save, O save them, make them joy - ful,
me - um
peo - ple;
In a - man - do Chris - tum
save, O save them, make them
me - um
peo - ple;
In a - man - do Chris - tum
save, O save them, make them
me - um
peo - ple;
In a - man - do Chris - tum
save, O save them, make them
me - um
peo - ple;
In a - man - do Chris - tum
save, O save them, make them

cres.
ut si - bi com - pla - - - - - - - -
and bless thine in - he - - - - - - - -
De - um,
joy - - ful,
cres.
De - um, ut si - bi com - pla - - - - - - - -
joy - ful, and bless thine in - he - - - - - - - -
cres.
De - um, ut si - bi com - pla - - -
joy - ful, and bless thine in - he - - -
cres.
De - um, ut si - bi com -
joy - ful, and bless thine in -
cres.
Allegro moderato. = 126.
sotto voce.
- - - - - - ce - am. In a - - man-do
- - - - - - ri - tance. Save them, save them
ff
sotto voce.
ut si - bi com - pla - ce - am. In a - - - man- do . . .
and bless thine in - he - ri - tance. Save, O . . . . save them, . . .
ff
sotto voce.
- - - - - - ce - am. In a - man- do . .
- - - - - - ri - tance. Save them, . . save them,
ff
sotto voce.
- - - - - - ce - am. In a - - man - do . .
- - - - - - ri - tance. Save them, . . save them, . .
ff
sotto voce.
- pla - - - - - ce - am. In a - - man - do. . .
- he - - - - - ri - tance. Save them, . . save them, . .
Allegro moderato.
ff
mf

Andante mosso. ♩ = 76.
Christum De-um, ut si - bi com
make them joy-ful, and bless thine in
Chris-tum . . . De - um, ut si - bi com - pla - ce -
make them . . . joy - ful, and bless thine in - he - ri -
Chris - tum De - um, ut si - bi com - pla - - ce -
make them joy - ful, and bless thine in - he - - ri -
Chris - tum De - um, ut si - bi com - pla - ce -
make them joy - ful, and bless thine in - he - - ri -
Chris - tum De - um, ut si - bi com - pla - - ce -
make them joy - ful, and bless thine in - he - - ri -
Andante mosso.
- pla - ce - am, ut si - bi com-pla - ce - am, fac ut ar - de - at cor
- he - ri -tance, and bless thine in - he - ri -tance. Lord! we pray thee, spare thy
- am, ut si - bi com - pla - ce - am,
- tance, and bless thine in - he - ri - tance,
- am, ut si - bi com - pla - ce - am,
- tance, and bless thine in - he - ri - tance,
- am, ut si - bi com - pla - ce - am, fac ut ar - de - at cor
- tance, and bless thine in - he - ri - tance, Lord! we pray thee, spare thy
- am, ut si - bi com - pla - ce - am,
- tance, and bless thine in - he - ri - tance,
ff

Adagio. sotto voce.
me-um in a-man-do Christum De-um, ut si-bi com-pla - - -
peo-ple; save, O save them, make them joy-ful, and bless thine in-he - - - -
sotto voce.
ut si-bi com-
and bless thine in-
sotto voce.
ut si-bi com
and bless thine in-
sotto voce.
me-um in a-man-do Chris-tum De-um, ut si-bi com-
peo-ple; save, O save them, make them joy-ful, and bless thine in-
ff
sotto voce.
in a-man-do Chris-tum De-um, ut si-bi com
save, O save them, make them joy-ful, and bless thine in-
Adagio.
p
Allegro moderato. = 126.
- - - - ce - am, in a - - mando Christum
- - - - ri - tance, save them, save them, make them
- - pla - ce - am, in a - - man-do . . . . Chris-tum . . .
- - he - ri - tance, save them, . . . save them, . . . make them . . .
- - pla - ce - am, in a - - man-do Chris-tum
- - he - ri - tance, save them, save them, make them
- - pla - ce - am, in a - - man-do Chris-tum
- - he - ri - tance, save them, save them, make them
- - pla - ce - am, in a - - man-do Chris-tum
- - he - ri - tance, save them, save them, make them
Allegro moderato.
mf

Andante mosso. ♩ = 76.
Deum, ut si - bi compla - ce-am,
joyful, and bless thine in - he - ritance,
De-um, ut si - bi com - pla - ce - am, ut si - bi com -
joy - ful, and bless thine in - he - ri - tance, and bless thine in -
De-um, ut si - bi com-pla - ce - am, ut si - bi com
joy - ful, and bless thine in - he - ri - tance, and bless thine in
De-um, ut si - bi com - pla - ce - am, ut si - bi com -
joy - ful, and bless thine in - he - ri - tance, and bless thine in -
De-um, ut si - bi com - pla - ce - am, ut si - bi com -
joy - ful, and bless thine in - he - ri - tance, and bless thine in -
Andante mosso.
ut si - bi com-pla - ce-am, fac ut ar - de - at cor me-um in a-man - do Chris-tum
and bless thine in - he - ritance. Lord! we pray thee, spare thy people; save, O save them, make them
- pla - ce - am, fac ut ar - de - at cor me-um in a-man - do Chris-tum
- he - ri - tance. Lord! we pray thee, spare thy people; save, O save them, make them
- pla - ce - am, in a-man - do Chris-tum
- he - ri - tance, save, O save them, make them
- pla - ce - am, fac ut ar - de - at cor me-um in a-man - do Chris-tum
- he - ri - tance. Lord! we pray thee, spare thy people; save, O save them, make them
- pla - ce - am, in a-man - do Chris-tum
- he - ri - tance, save, O save them, make them

Adagio. sotto voce.
De - um, ut si - bi com - pla - - - - - - - - - ce -
joy - ful, and bless thine in - he - - - - - - - - - ri -
sotto voce.
ut si - bi com - pla - - ce -
and bless thine in - he - - ri -
sotto voce.
sotto voce.
sotto voce.
Adagio.
p
- am, ut si - bi com - pla - ce - am. . .
- tance, and bless thine in - he - ri - tance. . .

No. 6. QUARTETT.—"SANCTA MATER, ISTUD AGAS."

(I HAVE LONGED FOR THY SALVATION.)

Andante.

PIANO. ♩= 69.

ff *pp*

TENOR.

Sanc - ta ma - ter, is - tud a - gas, cru - ci - fix - i fi - ge pla - gas,

I have long'd for thy sal - va - tion, and my hope was in thy goodness;

Con espress.

sanc - ta ma - ter, is - tud a - - gas, cru - ci - fix - i fi - ge

I have long'd for thy sal - va - - tion, and my hope was in thy

f *p*

pla - - gas Cor - de me - o, cor - de me - - - - o va - li -
good - - ness. Bless - ed be thy name, O Lord, . . . for e - -
- - de, cor - de me - o, cor - de me - o, cor - de
- - ver! Bless - ed be thy name, thy ho - ly name, O
me - o va - - - li - de.
Lord, for e - - - ver.
1st Treble.
Tu - i na - ti vul - ne -
Now and henceforth, we be -
f
p
ff
pp

ra - ti, tam dig - na - ti pro me pa - ti,
seech thee, turn our hearts to thy commandments,
TENOR.
Tu - i na - ti vul - ne - ra - ti, tam dig - na - ti pro me
Now and henceforth, we be - seech thee, turn our hearts to thy com -
tu - i na - ti vul - ne - ra - ti, tam dig - na - ti pro me
now and henceforth, we be - seech . . thee, turn our hearts to thy com -
pa - ti,
mandments,
pa - ti pœ - nas me - cum di - vi - de, ... di - vi -
mand - - ments, and in - cline them e - ver - more . . . to keep thy
de, pœ - nas . . me - cum, pœ - nas me - cum, pœ - nas
law, and in - cline them, and in - cline them e - ver -
pœ - nas mecum, pœ - nas me - cum, pœ - nas
and incline them, and in - cline them e - ver -

me - cum di - - vi - de.
- more to keep thy law.
me - cum di - - vi - de.
- more to keep thy law.
dolce.
p
Bass.
ff
Fac me ve - re te - cum
Give thy ser - vants un - der -
ff
2nd Treble.
ff
Fac . . . . . me ve - re te - cum fle - - - - re,
Give . . . . . thy ser - vants un - der - stand - - - - ing,
fle - - - re, cru - - - - ci - -
- stand - - - ing, so that
ff
p
ff
cru - - - - ci - fix - o con - do -
so . . . . that they may shun temp -
fix - o con - do - le - - - re,
they may shun temp - ta - - - tion,
ff
p

le - - re, do - nec e - go, do - -
ta - - tion, and in all things, and
de - nec e - go, do - -
and in all things, and
ff
pp
nec e - - go, do - - nec e - -
in all things, and in all
nec e - - go, do - - nec e - -
in all things, and in all
ff
go vix - - - - e - ro, . . do - nec . . e - go
things fol - - - - low thee, . . and in . . . all things
ff
go vix - - - - e - ro.
things fol - - - - low thee.
ff
p

1st Treble.
Jux - ta cru - cem te - cum
Oh! vouch-safe us true re -
vix - e - ro
fol - low thee.
Tenor.
Jux - ta cru - cem te - cum
Oh! vouch-safe us true re-
Bass.
Jux - ta cru - cem te - cum sta - re,
Oh! vouch - safe us true re - pen-tance,
pp
sta - re,
- pen-tance,
te li - ben - ter so - ci - a - re.
teach us al - ways to o - bey thee.
Te li - ben - ter so - ci - a - re,
Teach us al-ways to o - bey thee,
sta - re,
- pen-tance,
te li - ben - ter so - ci - a - re.
teach us al - ways to o - bey thee.
Jux - ta
Oh! vouch-

2nd Treble.
te li-ben-ter so-ci-a - - re,
teach us al-ways to o-bey . . thee,
cru-cem te-cum sta - re,
- safe us true re-pen - tance,
Bass.
in planc-tu de - si - de-ro, ... de - si - de-
and to walk the way of peace, ... the way of
2nd Treble.
In planc-tu de - si - de - ro, . . in planc -
and to walk the way of peace, . and to
Tenor.
In planc-tu, in planc - tu, in planc -
of peace, the way of peace, and to
- ro. In planc-tu, in planc - tu, in planc -
peace, of peace, the way of peace, and to
cres.

1st Treble,
p
in planctu, in
to walk the
f> f>
- tu de - si - de - ro, in planctu, in
walk the way of peace, to walk the
f> f>
- tu de - si - de - ro, in planctu, in
walk the way of peace, to walk the
f> f>
- tu de - si - de - ro, in planctu, in
walk the way of peace, to walk the
p
ff
planctu, in planc - tu de - si - de - ro.
way, and walk the way, the way . . of . . peace.
ff
planctu, in planc - tu de - si - de - ro.
way, and walk the way, the way . . of . . peace.
ff
planctu, in planc - tu de - si - de - ro.
way, and walk the way, the way . . of . . peace.
ff
planctu, in planc - tu de - si - de - ro.
way, and walk the way, the way . . of . . peace.
cres.
rf
ff
pp

sotto voce.
Vir - go, vir - gi - num præ - cla - ra, mi - hi jam non sis a - ma -
Let thy light so shine be - fore us, and thy mer - cy be up - on
- ra, Vir - go, vir - gi - num præ - cla - ra, mi - hi
us, let thy light so shine be - fore us, and thy

jam non sis a - ma - - ra, fac me te - - cum
mer - cy be up - on . . us, ev'n as is our
jam non sis a - ma - - ra, fac me te - - cum
mer - cy be up - on us, ev'n as is our
jam non sis a - ma - - ra, fac me te - - cum
mer - cy be up - on us, ev'n as is our
jam non sis a - ma - - ra, fac me te - - cum
mer - cy be up - on us, ev'n as is our
plan - - ge - re, ... fac me te - -
trust in thee, ... ev'n as is
plan - - ge - - re, ... fac me te - -
trust in thee, ... ev'n as is
plan - - ge - - re, ... fac me te - -
trust in thee, ... ev'n as is
plan - - ge - - re, ... fac me te - -
trust in thee, ... ev'n as is

cum plan - ge - re. . . . . . Vir - go, vir - gi-num præ
our trust in thee. . . . . . Let thy light so shine be -
cum plan - ge - re. . . . . .
our trust in thee. . . . . .
cum plan - ge - re. . . . . . Vir - go, vir - gi-num præ -
our trust in thee. . . . . . Let thy light so shine be -
cum plan - ge - re.
our trust in thee.
p
cla - ra, mi - hi jam non sis a - ma - ra,
fore us, and thy mer - cy be up - on us,
Vir - go, vir - gi - num præ - cla - ra, mi - hi jam non sis a -
Let thy light so shine be - fore us, and thy mer - cy be up -
cla - ra, mi - hi jam non sis a - ma - ra,
fore us, and thy mer - cy be up - on us,
Vir - go, vir - gi - num præ - cla - ra, mi - hi jam non sis a -
Let thy light so shine be - fore us, and thy mer - cy be up -

Vir - - go, vir - gi-num præ - cla - - ra, mi - hi jam non sis a -
let thy light so shine be - fore . . . us, and thy mer - cy be up -
- ma-ra,
- on us,
Vir - - go, vir - gi-num præ - cla - - ra, mi - - hi jam non sis a -
let thy light so snine be - fore . . . us, and thy mer - cy be up -
- ma-ra,
- on us,
- - ma - - ra, fac me te - cum plan - ge - re, ...
- - on . . . us, ev'n as is our trust in thee, ... our
- - ma - - ra, fac me te - cum plan - ge - re, ...
- - on . . . us, ev'n as is our trust in thee, ... our

plan - ge - re, fac me . . te - cum, fac me . . te - cum,
trust in thee, ev'n as . . is our trust in . . . thee, . .
fac me te-cum, fac me te - - cum,
ev'n as is our trust in thee,
plan - ge - re, fac me . . te - cum, fac me . . te - cum,
trust in thee, ev'n as . . is our trust in . . thee, . .
fac me te-cum, fac me te - cum,
ev'n as is our trust in thee,
fac me te - cum plan - - ge - re, fac me te-cum plan-ge -
ev'n as is our trust in thee, as is our trust in
fac me te - cum plan - - ge - re,
ev'n as is our trust in thee,
fac me te - cum plan - - ge - re, fac me te-cum plan-ge -
ev'n as is our trust in thee, ev'n as is our trust in
fac me te - cum plan - - ge - re,
ev'n as is our trust in thee,

pp
- - re,
thee,
plan - - ge-
as . . . our
p
fac me te-cum plan-ge - re, . .
ev'n as is our trust in thee,
plan - - ge-
as . . . our
- - re,
thee,
plan - - ge-
as . . . our
fac me te-cum plan-ge - re, . .
ev'n as is our trust in thee,
plan - - ge-
as . . . our
- re, . .
trust
plan - - - ge - re, . .
is still . . . in thee,
- re, . .
trust
plan - - - ge - re, . .
is still . . . in thee,
- - re, . .
trust
plan - - - ge - re, . .
is still . . . in thee,
- - re, . .
trust
plan - - - ge - re, . . plan - ge -
is still . . . in thee, is still in

te - - - - - - cum . . plan - - ge - -
as . . . . . our trust is still . . in . .

te - - - - - - cum . . plan - - ge - -
as . . . . . our trust is still . . in . .

te - - - - - - cum . . plan - - ge - -
as . . . . . our trust is still . . in . .

re, te - - - - - - cum plan - - ge - -
thee, as . . . . . our trust is still . . in . .

- re.
thee.

- re.
thee.

- re.
thee.

- re.
thee.

morendo.

No. 7. CAVATINA.—"FAC UT PORTEM."

(I WILL SING OF THY GREAT MERCY.)

Andante grazioso.
PIANO.
♪ = 104.
dolce.
dolce.
ff
ff
2nd TREBLE.
Fac ut por-tem Chris-ti mor-tem, pas-si-o-nis e-jus
I will sing of thy great mer-cy, for I was in deep af-
pp
sor-tem et pla-gas re-co-le-re, et
-fliction, and thou didst de-li-ver me, Lord,
f

pla-gas re
thou didst de
p
co - le - re
li - ver me!
ff pp ff pp ff pp
Fac me pla-gis vul - ne - ra - ri,
I will call un - to . . the peo - ple,
ff p ff pp
cru - ce hâc i - ne - - bri
and the na - tions all . . . shall
ff pp ff p

a - ri, ob a - mo - rem Fi - li - i, ob a -
hear me, and shall praise thy ho - ly name, and shall
- mo - rem Fi - li - i, ... ob a - morem Fi-li -
praise thy ho - ly name, . . . and shall praise thy ho-ly
- i, . . fac me pla-gis vul-ne - ra-ri, cru-ce hâc i - ne-bri -
name, . . I will call un - to the peo-ple, and the na - tions all shall
- a - ri, ob a - mo - rem Fi - li - i, ob . . . .
hear me, and shall praise thy ho - ly name, all . . . .
pp
pp
ff
f

a - mo - rem
shall praise thy
Fi - li - i, ob a - mo - rem
ho - ly name, all shall praise thy
Fi - li - i.
ho - ly name.

No. 8. Air and Chorus.—"INFLAMMATUS ET ACCENSUS."

(WHEN THOU COMEST.)

Vir - - go, sim de - fen - sus in di - - e ju -
- mem - - ber thou thy ser - vants, none else can de -

cres.

ff
- di - - - - - - - - - - - - ci - i.
- li - - - - - - - - - - - - ver us.

CHORUS. TREBLE.

ff
In di - e ju
None else can de -

ALTO.

ff
In di - e ju -
None else can de -

TENOR.

ff
In di - e ju -
None else can de -

BASS.

ff
In di - e ju -
None else can de -

ff

ff

- di - ci - i, in di - e ju - di - ci - i, in di - e ju -
- li - ver us, none else can de - li - ver us, none else can de -

- di - ci - i, in di - e ju - di - ci - i, in di - e ju -
- li - ver us, none else can de - li - ver us, none else can de -

- di - ci - i, in di - e ju - di - ci - i, in di - e ju -
- li - ver us, none else can de - li - ver us, none else can de -

- di - ci - i, in di - e ju - di - ci - i, in di - e ju -
- li - ver us, none else can de - li - ver us, none else can de -

- - di - ci - i, in di - e ju - di - ci - i.
- - li - ver us, none else can de - li - ver us.
- - di - ci - i, in di - e ju - di - ci - i.
- - li - ver us, none else can de - li - ver us.
- - di - ci - i, in di - e ju - di - ci - i.
- - li - ver us, none else can de - li - ver us.
- - di - ci - i, in di - e ju - di - ci - i.
- - li - ver us, none else can de - li - ver us.
pp
pp
SOLO. sotto voce.
Fac me cru - ce cus - to -
Save, and bring us to thy
3 3 3 3 3 3 3 3

- - di - - ri,
king - dom,
mor - - - te Chris- ti præ - mu -
there to wor - ship with the
sotto voce.
Fac me cru - - ce cus - - to - di - ri,
Save, and bring us to thy king-dom,
sotto voce.
Fac me cru - - ce cus - - to - di - ri,
Save, and bring us to thy king-dom,
sotto voce.
Fac me cru - - ce cus - - to - di - ri,
Save, and bring us to thy king-dom,
sotto voce.
Fac me cru - - ce cus - - to - di - ri,
Save, and bring us to thy king-dom,
- - ni - ri,
faith - ful,
mor - te Chris - - ti
there to wor - - ship
mor - - - te Chris - - ti præ - - mu - ni - ri,
there to wor - - ship with the faith - ful,
mor - te
there to
mor - - - te Chris - - ti præ - - mu - ni - ri,
there to wor - - ship with the faith - ful,
mor - te
there to
mor - - - te Chris - - ti præ - - mu - ni - ri,
there to wor - - ship with the faith - ful,
mor - te
there to
mor - - - te Chris - - ti præ - - mu - ni - ri,
there to wor - - ship with the faith - ful,
mor - te
there to

præ - mu- ni - - ri, con - fo- ve - - ri
with the faith - ful, and for e - - ver
Chris - ti præ - mu - ni - ri, con - fo -
wor - ship with the faith - ful, and for
gra - - - - - - - - - - - -
dwell . . . .
- ve - ri gra - ti - - - - â, con - fo -
e - ver dwell with thee, and for
tr
ff

ti - â.
with thee.
ve - ri gra - ti - â.
e - ver dwell with thee.
ve - ri gra - ti - â.
e - ver dwell with thee.
ve - ri gra - ti - â.
e - ver dwell with thee.
ve - ri gra - ti - â.
e - ver dwell with thee.
f
sotto voce.
In - - flam - ma - tus, in - flam-
When thou com - est, when thou
- ma - tus . . . et . . . ac - cen - sus per - te,
com - est . . . to . . . the judg - ment, Lord, re -
Vir - - go, sim de - fen - sus, per - te,
- mem - ber thou thy ser - vants, O re

Vir - - go, sim de - fen - sus in di - e ju -
- mem - - ber thou thy ser - vants! None else can de -
cres.
- di - - - - - - ci - i.
- li - - - - - ver us.
In di - e ju -
None else can de -
In di - e ju -
None else can de -
In di - e ju -
None else can de -
In di - e ju -
None else can de -
- di - ci - i, in di - e ju - di - ci - i,
- li - ver us, none else can de - li - ver us,
- di - ci - i, in di - e ju - di - ci - i,
- li - ver us, none else can de - li - ver us,
- di - ci - i, in di - e ju - di - ci - i,
- li - ver us, none else can de - li - ver us,
- di - ci - i, in di - e ju - di - ci - i,
- li - ver us, none else can de - li - ver us,

in di - e ju - di - ci - i, in di - e ju - di - ci
none else can de - li - ver us, none else can de - li - ver
in di - e ju - di - ci - i, in di - e ju - di - ci -
none else can de - li - ver us, none else can de - li - ver
in di - e ju - di - ci - i, in di - e ju - di - ci
none else can de - li - ver us, none else can de - li - ver
in di - e ju - di - ci - i, in di - e ju - di - ci
none else can de - li - ver us, none else can de - li - ver
- i.
us.
- i.
us.
- i.
us.
i.
us.
pp
pp

SOLO. sotto voce.
Fac me cru - ce cus - to di - - ri,
Save, and bring us to thy king - - dom,
sotto voce.
Fac me cru - ce cus - to -
Save, and bring us to thy
mor - - te Chris - ti præ - mu - ni - ri,
there to wor - ship with the faith - ful.
- di - ri,
king-dom,
mor - - - te Chris - ti præ - mu -
there to wor - ship with the

mor - te Chris - ti præ - mu ni - ri,
there to wor - ship with the faith - ful,
- ni - ri, mor - te Chris - ti præ - mu -
faith - ful, there to wor - ship with the
- ni - ri, mor - te Chris ti præ - mu -
faith - ful, there to wor - ship with the
- ni - ri, mor - te Chris - ti præ - mu
faith - ful, there to wor - ship with the
- ni - ri, mor - te Chris - ti præ - mu -
faith - ful, there to wor - ship with the
tr tr tr tr
con - fo - ve - ri gra - - - - - - - - -
and - for e - ver dwell
- ni - ri, con - fo - ve - ri gra - ti - - -
faith - ful, and for e - ver dwell with
- ni - ri, con - fo - ve - ri gra - ti - - -
faith - ful, and for e - ver dwell with
- ni - ri, con - fo - ve - ri gra - ti - - -
faith - ful, and for e - ver dwell with
- ni - ri, con - fo - ve - ri gra - ti - - -
faith - ful, and for e - ver dwell with

ff
ti -
with
-â, con - fo - - ve - - ri gra - ti -
thee, and for e - - ver dwell with
-â, con - fo - - ve - - ri gra - ti -
thee, and for e - - ver dwell with
-â, con - fo - - ve - - ri gra - ti -
thee, and for e - - ver dwell with
-â, con - fo - - ve - - ri gra - ti -
thee, and for e - - ver dwell with
ff
p
-â, con - fo -
thee, and for
-â, con - fo - ve - - - ri
thee, and for e - - - ver
-â, con - fo - ve - - - ri
thee, and for e - - - ver
-â, con - fo - ve - ri gra -
thee, and for e - ver dwell
-â, con - fo - ve - ri gra -
thee, and for e - ver dwell
ff

ve - ri gra - ti -
e - ver dwell . with
gra - ti
dwell with
gra - ti
dwell with
ti
with
ti
with
â, con - fo -
thee, and for
â, con - fo - ve - ri
thee, and for e - ver
â, con - fo - ve - ri
thee, and for e - ver
â, con - fo - ve - ri gra
thee, and for e - ver dwell
â, con - fo - ve - ri gra
thee, and for e - ver dwell
6

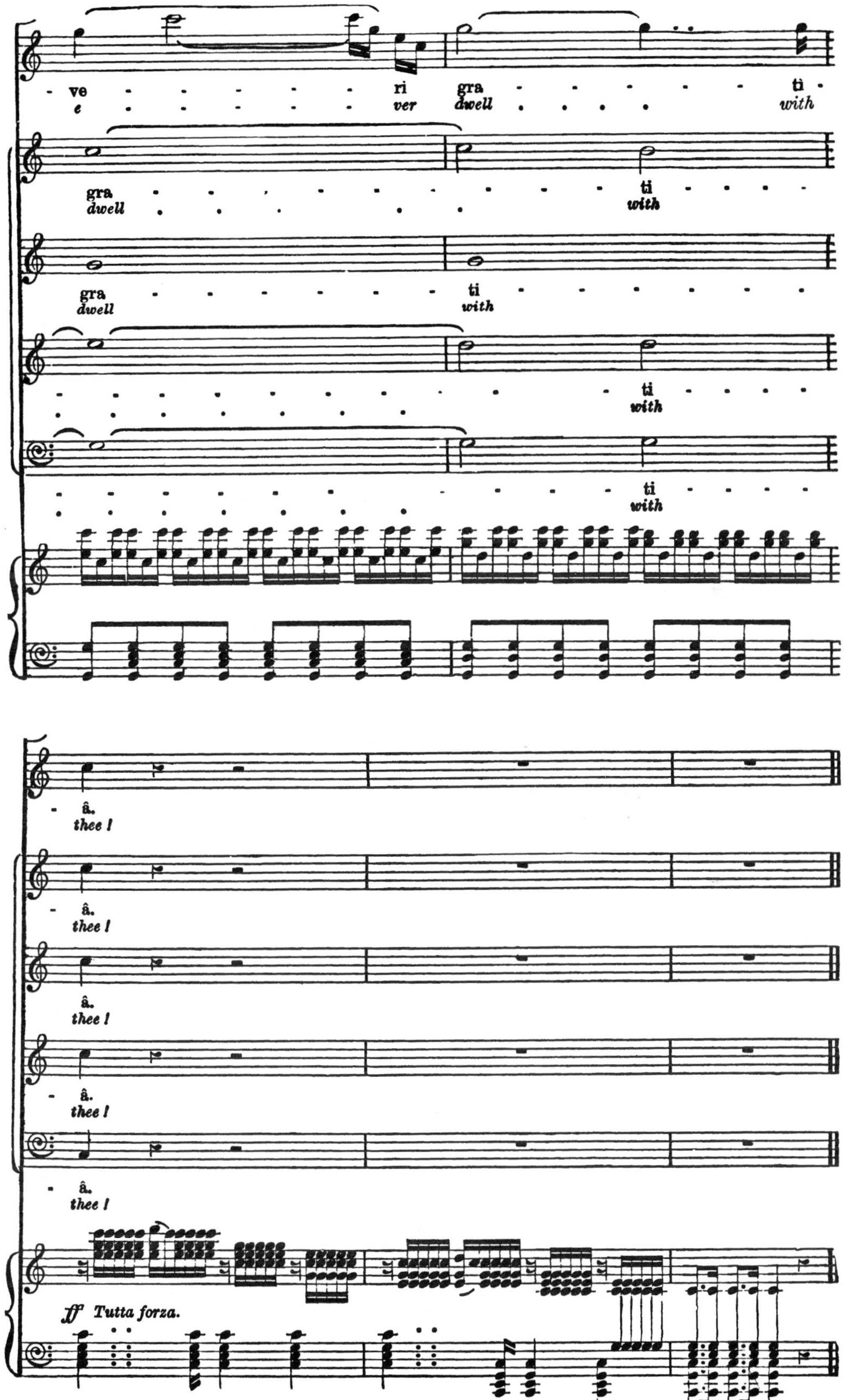
ve - - - - - - ri gra - - - - - - ti
e - - - - - - ver dwell - - - - - with
gra - - - - - - - - - - - ti - - - -
dwell - - - - - with
gra - - - - - - - ti - - - - - - -
dwell with
ti
with
ti
with
â.
thee !
â.
thee !
â.
thee !
â.
thee !
â.
thee !
ff Tutta forza.

No. 9.

QUARTET (*without accompaniment*).—" QUANDO CORPUS."

(HEAR US, LORD.)

- e - tur, fac ut a - ni - mæ do - ne - tur, a - ni - mæ do - ne - -
- deem - er and his great and won - d'rous mer - cies, all his won - d'rous mer -
- e - tur, fac ut a ni - mæ do - ne - tur, a - ni - mæ do - ne - -
- deem - er, and his great and won - d'rous mer - cies, all his won - d'rous mer -
- e - tur, fac ut a - ni - mæ do - ne - tur, a - ni - mæ do - ne - -
- deem - er, and his great and won - d'rous mer - cies, all his won - d'rous mer -
fac ut a - ni - mæ do - ne - tur, a - ni - mæ do - ne - -
and his great and won - d'rous mer - cies, all his won - d'rous mer -
ff
sotto voce.
- tur Pa - ra - di - si glo - ri - a. Quan - do
- cies, now and e - ver glo - ri - fy. Bless the
- tur, Pa - ra - di - si glo - ri - a. Quan - do
- cies, now and e - ver glo - ri - fy. Bless the
- tur, Pa - ra - di - si glo - ri - a. Quan - do
- cies, now and e - ver glo - ri - fy! Bless the
- tur, Pa - ra - di - si glo - ri - a. Quan - do
- cies, now and e - ver glo - ri - fy! Bless the
p

cor - pus mo - ri - e - tur, fac ut a - ni - mæ do - ne - tur Pa - ra -
name of our Re - deem - er, and his great and won - d'rous mer - cies, now and
cor - pus mo - ri - e - tur, fac ut a - ni - mæ do - ne - tur Pa - ra -
name of our Re - deem - er, and his great and won - d'rous mer - cies, now and
cor - pus mo - ri - e - tur, fac ut a - ni - mæ do - ne - tur Pa - ra -
name of our Re - deem - er, and his great and won - d'rous mer - cies, now and
cor - pus mo - ri - e - tur, fac ut a - ni - mæ do - ne - tur Pa - ra -
name of our Re - deem - er, and his great and won - d'rous mer - cies, now and
pp
sotto voce.
- di - si, Pa - ra - di - si glo - ri - a. Quan - do
e - ver, now and e - ver glo - ri - fy! All . . . his
sotto voce.
- di - si, Pa - ra - di - si glo - ri - a. Quan - do
e - ver, now and e - ver glo - ri - fy! All . . . his
sotto voce.
- di - si, Pa - ra - di - si glo - ri - a. Quan - do
e - ver, now and e - ver glo - ri - fy! All . . . his
sotto voce.
di - si, Pa - ra - di - si glo - ri - a. Quan do
e - ver, now and e - ver glo - ri - fy! All . his
pp
p

cor - pus mo - ri - e - tur, fac . . ut a - ni
mer - cies, all . . his mer - cies, all . . his great and
cor - pus mo - ri - e - tur, fac . . ut a - ni -
mer - cies, all . . his mer - cies, all . . his great and
cor - pus mo - ri - e - tur, fac . . ut a - ni -
mer - cies, all . . his mer - cies, all . . his great and
cor - pus mo - ri - e - tur, fac . . ut a - ni -
mer - cies, all . . his mer - cies, all . . his great and
- mæ do - ne - tur Pa - ra - di - si glo - ri - a.
won - d'rous mer - cies, now and e - ver glo - ri - fy!
- mæ do - ne - tur Pa - ra - di - si glo - ri - a.
won - d'rous mer - cies, now and e - ver glo - ri - fy
- mæ do - ne - tur Pa - ra - di - si
won - d'rous mer - cies, now and e - ver
- mæ do - ne - tur Pa - ra - di - si
won - d'rous mer - cies, now and e - ver

sotto voce.
Quan- do cor - pus mo - ri - e - tur, fac ut a - ni - mæ do -
Bless the name of our Re - deem - er, and his great and won - d'rous
sotto voce.
Quan- do cor - pus mo - ri - e - tur, fac ut a - ni - mæ do -
Bless the name of our Re - deem - er, and his great and won - d'rous
ff
sotto voce.
glo - ri - a. Quan- do cor - pus mo - ri - e - tur, fac ut a - ni - mæ do -
glo - ri - fy! Bless the name of our Re - deem - er, and his great and won - d'rous
ff
sotto voce.
glo - ri - a. Quan- do cor - pus mo - ri - e - tur, fac ut a - ni - mæ do -
glo - ri - fy! Bless the name of our Re - deem - er, and his great and won - d'rous
ff
p
pp
- ne - tur Pa - ra - di - si, Pa - ra - di - si glo - ri - a. Quan - do
mer - cies now and e - ver, now and e - ver glo - ri - fy, all his
pp
- ne - tur Pa - ra - di - si, Pa - ra - di - si glo - ri - a. Quan - do
mer - cies now and e - ver, now and e - ver glo - ri - fy, all his
pp
- ne - tur Pa - ra - di - si, Pa - ra - di - si glo - ri - a. Quan - do
mer - cies now and e - ver, now and e - ver glo - ri - fy, all his
pp
- ne - tur Pa - ra - di - si, Pa - ra - di - si glo - ri - a. Quan - do
mer - cies now and e - ver, now and e - ver glo - ri - fy, all his
pp

cor-pus mo-ri-e-tur, fac ut a - ni-mæ do-ne - - -
mer-cies, all his mer-cies, all his great . . and won-d'rous mer - - -
cor-pus mo-ri-e-tur, fac ut a - - ni - mæ do-ne
mer-cies, all his mer-cies, all his great and won-d'rous mer
cor-pus mo-ri-e-tur, fac ut a - - ni - mæ do-ne
mer-cies, all his mer-cies, all his great and won-d'rous mer
cor-pus mo-ri-e-tur, fac ut a - - ni - mæ do-ne
mer-cies, all his mer-cies, all his great and won-d'rous mer
sotto voce.
- tur Pa-ra-di-si, Pa-ra-di-si glo - ri - a. Quan-do
- cies now and e-ver, now and e-ver glo - ri - fy, all his
- tur Pa-ra-di-si, Pa-ra-di-si glo - ri - a. Quan-do
- cies now and e-ver, now and e-ver glo - ri - fy, all his
- tur Pa-ra-di-si, Pa-ra-di-si glo - ri - a. Quan-do
- cies now and e-ver, now and e-ver glo - ri - fy, all his
- tur Pa-ra-di-si, Pa-ra-di-si glo-ri - a. Quan-do
- cies now and e-ver, now and e-ver glo-ri - fy, all his

ff
cor - pus mo - ri - e - tur, fac ut a - ni - mæ do - ne - - -
mer - cies, all his mer - cies, all his great . . and wond'rous mer - -
ff
cor - pus mo - ri - e - tur, fac ut a - - ni - mæ do - ne -
mer - cies, all his mer - cies, all his great and wond'rous mer -
ff
cor - pus mo - ri - e - tur, fac ut a - - ni - mæ do - ne -
mer - cies, all his mer - cies, all his great and wond'rous mer -
ff
cor - pus mo - ri - e - tur, fac ut a - - ni - mæ do - ne -
mer - cies, all his mer - cies, all his great and wond'rous mer -
ff
ff
sotto voce.
- tur Pa - ra - di - si, Pa - ra - di si glo - - ri - a,
- cies now and e - ver, now and e ver glo - - ri - fy,
ff
sotto voce.
- tur Pa - ra - di - si, Pa - ra - di - si glo - - ri - a,
- cies now and e - ver, now and e - ver glo - - ri - fy,
ff
sotto voce.
- tur Pa - ra - di - si, Pa - ra - di - si glo - - ri - a,
- cies now and e - ver, now and e - ver glo - - ri - fy,
ff
sotto voce.
- tur Pa - ra - di - si, Pa - ra - di - si glo - ri - a, Pa - ra -
- cies now and e - ver, now and e - ver glo - ri - fy, now and
ff
p

Pa - ra - di - si, Pa - ra
now and e - ver, now and
Pa - ra - di - si glo
now and e - ver glo
Pa - ra - di - si, Pa - ra - di - si glo
now and e - ver, now and e - ver glo
di - si, glo - ri - a, Pa - ra - di - si glo
e - ver glo - ri - fy, now and e - ver glo
di - si, Pa - ra - di - si, Pa - ra - di - si, Pa - ra - di - si... glo - ri - a.
e - ver, now and e - ver, now and e - ver, now and e - ver.. glo - ri - fy!
ri - a.
ri - fy!
ri - a.
ri - fy!
ri - a.
ri - fy!
tr......
f

No. 10. CHORUS.—"IN SEMPITERNA SÆCULA, AMEN."

(TO HIM BE GLORY EVERMORE.)

f
In sem-pi-ter - na sæ - cu - la, a
To him be glo - ry e - ver - more, a
f
a
a
f
men, a
men, a
f
In sem-pi-ter - na sæ - cu - la, a
To him be glo - ry e - ver-more, a
men, a
men, a
f
a
a

men, a
men, a
men, a
men, a
men, in sem-pi-ter - na sæ-cu-la, a
men, to him be glo - ry e-ver-more, a
men, a
men, a
men, a
men, a
men, a
men, a
men, a
men, a
men, in sempi-ter - na sæ-cu-la, a
men, to him be glo - ry e-ver-more, a

- men, in sem-pi - ter - na sæ - cu - la, ... a - - men, a-men,
- men, to him be glo - ry e - ver - more, ... a - - men, a-men,
- men, a-men, in sem-pi - ter - na sæ - cu -
- men, a-men, to him be glo - ry e - ver -
- men, in sem-pi - ter-na sæ - cu - - la, in sem-pi - ter-na sæ -
- men, to him be glo-ry e - ver - - more. to him be glo-ry e -
- - - - - - - - - men, a - - - - - - men,
- - - - - - - - - men, a - - - - - - men,
in sem-pi - ter - - na sæ - cu - la, ... a - - men, a-men,
to him be glo - - ry e - ver - more, . . . a - - men, a-men,
- la, . . . a - men, a - men, in sem-pi - ter - na sæ - cu -
- more, . . a - men, a - men, to him be glo - ry e - ver -
- cu - - la, in sem-pi - ter-na sæ - cu - - la, in sem-pi - ter-na sæ -
- ver - - more, to him be glo - ry e - - ver-more, to him glo - ry e -
a - - - - - - - - men, a - - - - - - - men,
a - - - - - - - - men, a - - - - - - - men,

in sem-pi - ter - na sæ - cu - la, . . . in sem-pi- ter - na
to him be glo - ry e - ver - more, . . to him be glo - ry
- la, . . . a - men, a-men, in sem-piter - na, a - - - - -
- more, . . a - men, a - men, to him be glo - ry, a - - - - -
- cu - - la, in sem-pi - ter - na, sæ - cu - - la a - - - - - men,
- ver - - more, to him be glo - ry e - ver - - more, a - - - - - men,
a - - - - - - - - - - men, a - - - - - - - - - -
a - - - - - - - - - - men, a - - - - - - - - - -
sæ - cu - la, a - - - - - - - - - - - - - - men, a - - -
e - ver -more, a - - - - - - - - - - - - - - men, a - - -
- - - - - - - - - - - - - - - - - men, in sem-pi-ter - na
- - - - - - - - - - - - - - - - - men, to him be glo - ry
a - - - - - - - - - - - - - - - - men, a - - - -
a - - - - - - - - - - - - - - - - men, a - - - -
- - - - - - - - - - - - - - - - - men,
- - - - - - - - - - - - - - - - - men,

men, in sem-pi-ter - na
men, to him be glo - ry
sæ-cu-la, a - - - - - - - - - men,
e-vermore, a - - - - - - - - - men,
men, in sem-pi-
men, to him be
a
a
sæ - cu - la, ... a - men, a-men, in sem-pi-ter - na
e - ver - more, ... a - men, a-men, to him be glo - ry
a-men, in sem-pi-ter - na sæ - cu - la, . . a -
a-men, to him be glo - ry e - ver - more, . . a -
-ter-na sæ - cu - - la, in sempi-ter-na sæ - cu - - la, in sempi-
glo-ry e - ver - - more, to him be glo-ry e - ver - - more, to him be
- men, a - - - - - - men, a - - -
- men, a - - - - - - men, a - - -

sæ - cu - la, . . . a - - - - - men, a - - - - -
e - ver - more, . . . a - - - - - men, a - - - - -
- men, a - men, in sem-pi - ter - na sæ - - cu - - la, ...
- men, a - men, to him be glo - ry e - - ver - - more, ...
- ter - na sæ - cu - - la, in sem-pi - ter - na sæ - cu - la, a -
glo - ry e - ver - - more, to him be glo - ry e - ver - more, a
- - - men, a - - - - - men, a - - - - - - -
- - - men, a - - - - - men, a - - - - - - -
- - - - - - - - men, a - - - - - - - - -
- - - - - - - - men, a - - - - - - - - -
. . . . a - - - - - - - men, a - - -
. . . . a - - - - - - - men, a - - -
- - - - - - - - men, a - - - - - - - - -
- - - - - - - - men, a - - - - - - - - -
- - - - - - - - men, in sem pi - ter - na sæ - cu - la, a
- - - - - - - - men, to him be glo - ry e - ver-more, a

men, in sem-pi - ter - na, in sempi-ter
men, to him be glo - ry, to him be glo
men, a - men, a - men, a - men, a
men, a - men, a - men, a - men, a
men, in sem-pi - ter - na, in sempi - ter
men, to him be glo - ry, to him be glo
men, a - men, a - men, a - men, a
men, a - men, a - men, a - men, a
ff
na, in sempi-ter - na, in sempi-ter - na, a
ry, to him be glo - ry, to him be glo - ry, a
men, a - men, a
men, a - men, a
na, in sempi-ter - na, in sempi-ter - na, a
ry, to him be glo - ry, to him be glo - ry, a
men, a
men, a
pp

men, in sem- pi - ter - na
men, to him be glo ry
men, in sem-pi -
men, to him be
men,
men,
men,
men,
p

sæ - - - - - - - - cu - la, a - - - - - - -
e - - - - - - - - ver-more, a - - - - - - -
- ter - na sæ - - - - - - - cu-la, a - - - -
glo - ry e - - - - - - - vermore, a - - - -
in sem-pi-ter - na sæ - - - - - - - cu - la, . .
to him be glo - ry e - - - - - - - ver - more,
in sem-pi - ter - na sæ - cu - la, ... a - - -
to him be glo - ry e - ver - more, ... a - - -
cres. . . . . f ff
- - men, a - - - - - - - men, a - - -
- - men, a - - - - - - - men, a - - -
- - - - - - men, a - - - - - - -
- - - - - - men, a - - - - - - -
a - - - - - - - - - - - - men,
a - - - - - - - - - - - - men,
- - - - - - - - - - - men, a - -
- - - - - - - - - - - men, a - -

men, in sem-pi-ter-na, in sempi-ter-na,
men, to him be glo-ry, to him be glo-ry,
men, a-men, in sem-pi-ter-na, in sempi-ter-na,
men, a-men, to him be glo-ry, to him be glo-ry,
a-men, in sem-pi-ter-na, in sempi-ter-na,
a-men, to him be glo-ry, to him be glo-ry,
men, a-men, in sem-pi-ter-na, in sem-pi-
men, a-men, to him be glo-ry, to him be
p
in sem-pi-ter-na, in sem-pi-ter-na, in sempi-ter-
to him be glo-ry, to him be glo-ry, to him be glo-
in sem-pi-ter-na, in sem-pi-ter-na, in sem-pi-
to him be glo-ry, to him be glo-ry, to him be
in sem-pi-ter-na, in sem-pi-ter-na,
to him be glo-ry, to him be glo-ry,
ter-na, in sem-pi-ter-na, a-men,
glo-ry, to him be glo-ry, a-men,
cres. f
ff

na, a men, in sem-pi-ter na
ry, a men, to him be glo ry
ter na, a men, in sem-pi
glo ry, a men, to him be
in sem-pi-ter na, a men,
to him be glo ry, a men,
in sempi ter na, a men,
to him be glo ry, a men,
p
sæ cu-la, a
e ver-more, a
ter na sæ cu-la, a
glo ry e vermore, a
in sem-pi-ter na sæ cu-la,
to him be glo ry e ver-more,
in sem-pi-ter na sæ-cu la, a
to him be glo ry e ver more, a
cres.
f
ff
ff

- - - men, a - - - - - - - - - - - - men, a - - - -
- - - men, a - - - - - - - - - - - - men, a - - -
- - - - - - - - - - - men, a - - - - - - - - - - -
- - - - - - - - - - - men, a - - - - - - - - - - -
a - - - - - - - - - - - - - - - - - men,
a - - - - - - - - - - - - - - - - - men,
- - - - - - - - - - - - - - - men, a - - - -
- - - - - - - - - - - - - - - men, a - - -
- - - - - - - - - men, in sempi-ter - na, in sempi-ter - na,
- - - - - - - - - men, to him be glo - ry, to him be glo - ry,
- - men, a - - - men, in sempi-ter - na, in sempi-ter - na,
- - men, a - - - men, to him be glo - ry, to him be glo - ry,
a - - - - - - - - men, in sempi-ter - na, in sempi-ter - na,
a - - - - - - - - men, to him be glo - ry, to him be glo - ry,
- - - - - - - men, a - men, in sem-pi - ter - na, in sem - pi -
- - - - - - - men, a - men, to him be glo - ry, to him be
p

in sem-pi - ter - na, in sem-pi - ter - - - na, in sem-pi - ter - -
to him be glo - ry, to him be glo - - - ry, to him be glo - -
in sem-pi - ter - na, in sem-pi - ter - - na, in sem-pi -
to him be glo - ry, to him be glo - - - ry, to him be
in sem-pi - ter - na, in sem-pi - ter - - - na,
to him be glo - ry, to him be glo - - - ry,
- ter - na, in sem - pi - ter - na, a - - men,
glo - ry, to him be glo - ry, a - - men,
cres.
f
ff
na, a - - - - - - men, in sem - pi - ter - - -
ry, a - - - - - - men, to him be glo - - -
- ter - - - - - - - - - na, a - - - men, a - men, a - -
glo - - - - - - - - - ry, a - - - men, a - men, a - -
in sem-pi-ter - - - - - - na, a - - - men, in sem-pi - ter - - -
to him be glo - - - - - - ry, a - - - men, to him be glo - - -
in sem-pi - ter - na, a - - - men, a - men, a - -
to him be glo - ry, a - - - men, a - men, a - -
ff

na, in sem-pi-ter - - na, in sem-pi-ter - - na, in sem-pi-ter - -
ry, to him be glo - - ry, to him be glo - - ry, to him be glo - -
men, a - men, a - - - - - - - - - - - -
men, a - men, a - - - - - - - - - - - -
na, in sem-pi-ter - - na, in sem-pi-ter - - na, in sem-pi-ter - -
ry, to him be glo - - ry, to him be glo - - ry, to him be glo - -
men, a - men, a - - - - - - - - - - - -
men, a - men, a - - - - - - - - - - - -
Andantino moderato. ♪= 132.
na,
ry,
men,
men,
na,
ry,
men,
men,
Andantino moderato.
pp

sotto voce.
a - men,
a - men,
a -
a -
sotto voce.
a - men,
a - men,
a -
a -
sotto voce.
a - men,
a - men,
a -
a -
sotto voce.
a - men,
a - men,
a -
a -
pp
p
- men,
- men,
a - - - men,
a - - - men,
a - - - - - -
a - - - - - -
pp

Tempo 1mo. Animato.
men, in sem-pi - ter - - - - - - - na, in sem-pi - ter - - -
men, to him be glo - - - - - - - ry, to him be glo - - -
men, a - - - - - - - - - - - - - -
men, a
men, in sem-pi - ter - - - - - - -
men, to him be glo - - - - - - -
men, a - - - - - - - - - - - - - -
men, a
Tempo 1mo. Animato.
na,
ry,
na, in sem-pi - ter - - - - - - - - - na,
ry, to him be glo - - - - - - - - - ry,

a - - - - - - - men, in sempi - ter - - - - - - - -
a - - - - - - - men, to him be glo - - - - - - - -
men, a - - - - - - -
men, a - - - - - - -
a - - - - - - - men, in sempi - ter - -
a - - - - - - - men, to him be glo - -
men, a - - - - - -
men, a - - - - - -
- - na, in sempi - ter - - - - - - - - - na,
- - ry, to him be glo - - - - - - - - - ry,
na, in sempi - ter - - - - - na,
ry, to him be glo - - - - - ry,

Novello Publishing Limited
Printed in Great Britain by Caligraving Limited, Thetford, Norfolk.